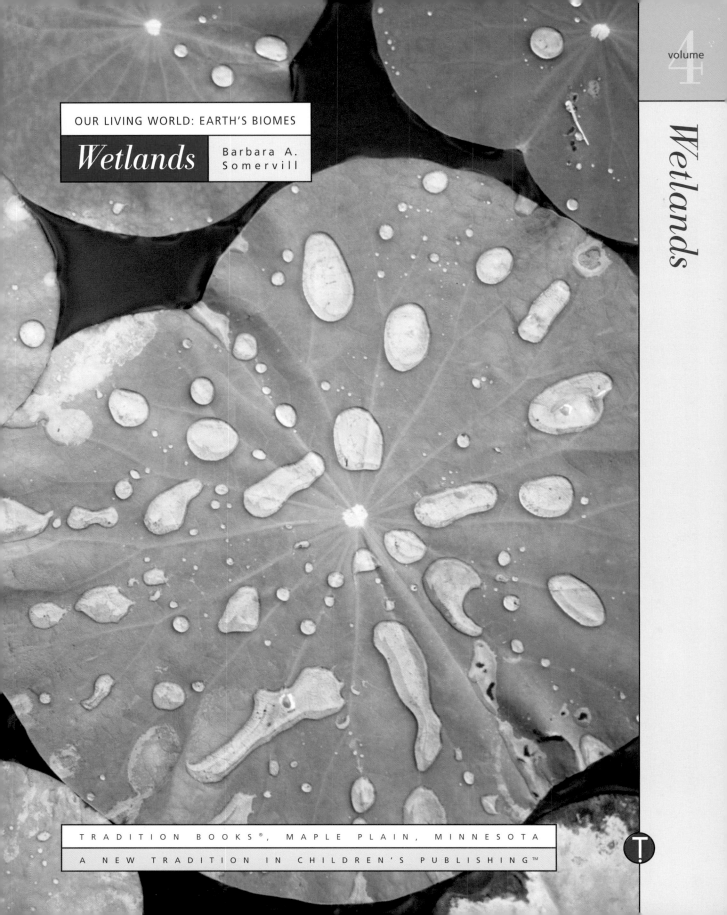

OUR LIVING WORLD: EARTH'S BIOMES

Wetlands

Barbara A. Somervill

volume 4

Wetlands

TRADITION BOOKS®, MAPLE PLAIN, MINNESOTA

A NEW TRADITION IN CHILDREN'S PUBLISHING™

ABOUT THE AUTHOR

Barbara A. Somervill is the author

of many books for children. She loves

learning and sees every writing

project as a chance to learn new

information or gain a new under-

standing. Ms. Somervill grew up in

New York State, but has also lived in

Toronto, Canada; Canberra, Australia;

California; and South Carolina. She

currently lives with her husband in

Simpsonville, South Carolina.

CONTENT ADVISER

Susan Woodward, Professor of

Geography, Radford University,

Radford, Virginia

In gratitude to George R. Peterson Sr. for introducing me to the beauty of creation
—George R. Peterson Jr., Publisher, Tradition Books®

Published in the United States of America by Tradition Books® and distributed to the school and library market by The Child's World®

[ACKNOWLEDGMENTS]
For Editorial Directions, Inc.: E. Russell Primm, Editorial Director; Dana Meachen Rau, Line Editor; Katie Marsico, Associate Editor; Judi Shiffer, Associate Editor and Library Media Specialist; Matthew Messbarger, Editorial Assistant; Susan Hindman, Copy Editor; Lucia Raatma, Proofreaders; Ann Grau Duvall, Peter Garnham, Deborah Grahame, Katie Marsico, Elizabeth K. Martin, and Kathy Stevenson, Fact Checkers; Tim Griffin/IndexServ, Indexer; Cian Loughlin O'Day, Photo Researcher; Linda S. Koutris, Photo Selector

For The Design Lab: Kathleen Petelinsek, design, art direction, and cartography; Kari Thornborough, page production

[PHOTOS]
Cover/frontispiece: Paul Edmondson/Corbis.
Interior: Animals Animals/Earth Scenes: 26 (Maresa Pryor), 73 (Fred Whitehead), 78 (Michael Fogden), 82 (Peter Weimann), 85 (McDonald Wildlife Photography), 89 (Gordon & Cathy Illg), 90 (Allen Blake Sheldon); Erwin & Peggy Bauer: 37; Corbis: 8 (Richard Cummins), 19 (Galen Rowell), 28 (Mark Jones), 36 (Paul A. Souders), 39 (Peter Johnson), 53 (Kevin Fleming), 64 (Brandon D. Cole), 72 (George D. Lepp), 83 (Gary Braasch), 86 (Bettmann), 88 (Jonathan Blair); Digital Vision: 14; Raymond Gehman/Corbis: 38, 67, 76, 81; Getty Images/ Brand X Pictures: 4, 24, 79; Randall Hyman: 42; Adam Jones/Dembinsky Photo Associates: 11, 51; Wolfgang Kaehler: 48; Dwight R. Kuhn: 41, 54, 69; Frans Lanting/Minden Pictures: 18, 33; Joe McDonald/Corbis: 27, 70; Joe McDonald/Tom Stack & Associates: 65; Barry Mansell/Naturepl.com: 44; Anthony Mercieca/Dembinsky Photo Associates: 61; Minden Pictures: 7 (Tui De Roy), 34 (Tim Fitzharris); David Muench/Corbis: 47, 75; Papilio/Corbis: 55 (Frank Young), 56 (Clive Druett); Photodisc: 10, 20, 21, 22, 30, 58, 62; Marie Read: 77; James P. Rowan: 17; Sydney Catchment Authority: 45, 46; Gerald D. Tang: 12.

[LIBRARY OF CONGRESS CATALOGING-IN-PUBLICATION DATA]
CIP data available

Table of Contents

Defining Wetlands

A flurry of gray and beige wings flutter over Nebraska's Platte River wetlands every year just before spring. About 75 percent of North America's sandhill cranes (nearly half a million cranes) gather there for four to six weeks. They come to stuff themselves on corn before flying to the Arctic.

▲ North America's Platte River wetlands

Regional farmers harvest their corn crops by machine. Harvesters miss some corn. Cattle feed on missed ears of corn, but they drop some kernels. When the cranes arrive each February and March, they feast on kernels left in the fields. Farmers estimate that the cranes eat about 1,500 tons of corn yearly.

The sandhill cranes lift off again in April. They fly at heights of up to 13,000 feet (3,962 meters). Their 6-foot (1.8-m) wings carry them north to nesting sites on **tundra** wetlands. Nebraska corn fuels the cranes for the two months of flying it takes to reach the Arctic.

Freshwater Wetlands

Wetlands are easy to identify. Cover solid land with 1 foot (.3 m) of water, and the land becomes wetlands. The soil becomes sloppy, mucky, and squishy. About 6 percent of all land is covered by wetlands. These include swamps and bogs, marshes and fens.

The source of water determines the type of wetlands that develop. Some

? WORDS TO KNOW . . .

tundra (TUHN-druh) treeless areas found in the Arctic or on high mountains

◀ A sandhill crane takes flight above a nature preserve.

wetlands collect water from rain and snow. Some get water from underground springs or rivers. Others collect surface water from **runoff** or floods. About 94 percent of wetlands in the United States hold freshwater.

Climate influences the animals and plants found in wetlands. Arctic tundra wetlands provide nesting sites for millions of migrating birds each summer. Arctic plants are mostly low-lying

▲ South America's Amazon River basin

lichens, mosses, and sedges. Tropical wetlands, such as much of the Amazon River **basin,** have warm weather and daily rainfall. Insects, birds, **reptiles,** and **amphibians** live there all year. Grasses and flowering plants grow over every acre of land all year as well.

Wetlands perform services in nature. They filter pollution and raw **sewage** from water. Sometimes a wetland

environment can clean the water by absorbing pollutants before the water enters our lakes, rivers, and streams. Nature also uses wetlands as a nursery for animal species. Ducks, geese, and more than 100 other kinds of birds breed in wetlands.

Bogs, Pocosins, and Fens

Bogs form when sphagnum moss slowly covers a lake or pond from the edge to the center. Bog water comes from the rain or melted snow. As the moss dies, it sinks to the pond floor. The dead moss forms peat because of acidic water conditions and a lack of oxygen. Water gets oxygen from springs, the plant life, and movement such as rapids.

Newfoundland, Canada, features ▶ many tundra marshes.

▲ This peat will be dried and then burned to provide heat for families in County Kerry, Ireland.

Still water has little oxygen.

Bogs are found throughout the world. In the United States, bogs are common in the northeast and northern Midwest. Bogs support moose, deer, beavers, lynx, otters, and minks. Migratory birds, such as sandhill cranes and short-eared owls, need bogs for nesting sites. The main plant in bogs is sphagnum moss.

Pocosin is a Native American term. It is Algonquian for "hilltop swamp." The main plants in this swamp are evergreen shrubs. A pocosin's water comes from rain or melted snow. Pocosins are found only along the Atlantic coast in

> **! WOULD YOU BELIEVE?**
>
> Sphagnum moss holds many times its own weight in water. Native Americans used the moss for diapers. In World War I, it was used to bandage wounds.

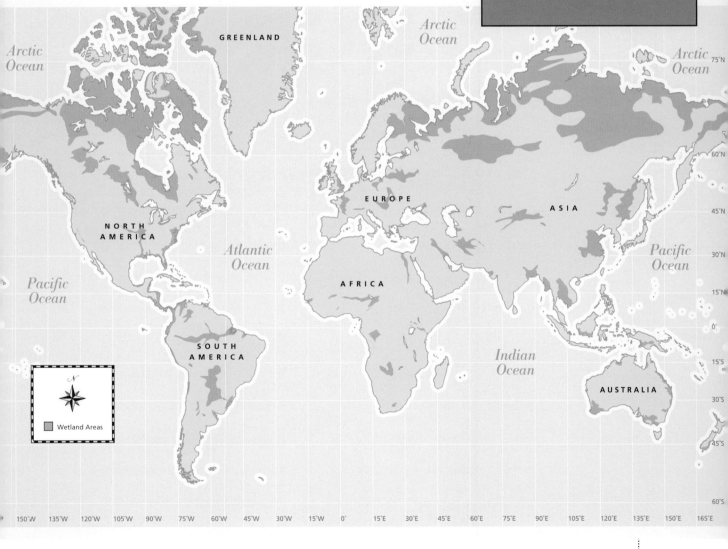

▲ Wetlands in Africa, Asia, Australia, Europe, North America, and South America

▲ A black bear cub seeks berries and roots in a bog.

Virginia, the Carolinas, and northern Florida.

Fens are wetlands with a regular freshwater supply. Water levels remain regular in fens. Quick-growing grasses and sedges make many fens look like meadows. Large fens provide habitats for moose, deer, black bears, lynx, hares and rabbits, otters, and minks.

Cranes, owls, and sparrows make their homes in fens.

Some fish may live in a fen, particularly if a stream feeds the wetland. Typical fen fish species include pike, bluegill, bass, and trout. In warm regions, snakes, turtles, toads, frogs, and lizards may live in these wetlands.

Summer finds this marsh green and healthy. ▶

Freshwater Marshes

The term *marsh* covers a wide range of very different wetlands. Freshwater marsh-lands range from hot tropical river basins to the freezing Arctic tundra.

Rivers, streams, lakes, or **groundwater** feed freshwater marshes. Marshes form when rivers or lakes overrun their banks. Water cover measures from 6 inches (15 centimeters) to about 3 feet (1 m). The water levels change with the seasons and weather and are affected by floods or heavy rainfall.

> **? WORDS TO KNOW . . .**
>
> **groundwater (ground-WAW-tur)** water that exists in bedrock below the surface of the earth

▲ Wet meadows come alive with wildflowers from spring through autumn.

Cypress and willow trees line the margins between rivers or lakes and the marshlands. The marshes contain mostly grasses and nonwoody plants. Grasses sprout up in the muck. Wild irises, orchids, and pale yellow goldenrod sprinkle marshes with color.

Wet Meadows and Prairie Potholes

Some wetlands last only as long as it takes for the water they hold to **evaporate.** They are seasonal wetlands and are active usually during winter and spring. By summer, the water has dried up. Temporary wetlands include wet meadows and some prairie potholes. Plants are mostly grasses and wildflowers.

Melting snow and heavy spring rains create wet meadows and prairie potholes. Wet meadows are generally grassy fields with poor water drainage. Water sits on the ground, making it soggy.

Prairie potholes form the same way as wet meadows, only they are shallow basins, not flat land. About 10,000 years ago as the Ice Age ended, glacial ice melted, leaving depressions in the ground. These depressions later filled with water, becoming potholes or kettles. Many

? WORDS TO KNOW . . .

evaporate (i-VAP-uh-rate) to change from a liquid to a gas

📖 READ IT!

Wetlands: The Web of Life by Paul Rezendes (Verve Editions, 1996) presents the stunning beauty of swamps, bogs, and prairie potholes.

? WORDS TO KNOW . . .

ecosystem (EE-koh-siss-tuhm) a community of plants and animals and their relationship with the surrounding environment

of these holes lie in the prairies of the northern Great Plains in the United States. The potholes fill with snow and water, creating a part-time wetland **ecosystem.**

Seasonal wetlands are like truck stops for migrating birds. Millions of ducks, geese, cranes, swans, and plovers set down for the night in these springtime wetlands. There, they feed on frogs, toads, and swarms of insects. Seed and plant eaters feast on the grasses and wildflowers.

▲ White-faced ducks build their nests in wetlands. Their young flourish in a marshy habitat.

▲ Southeastern U.S. swamps

Some Freshwater, Some Salt Water

ᐧᑌ Swamps and bayous feature more trees and shrubs than bogs, fens, or meadows. Within one swamp, there may be forests, grasslands, wildflower meadows, ponds, and rivers. Swamps exist on most continents. Water may come from underground springs, rivers, rainfall, or other sources. Swamp and bayou

PROFILE: CONGO RIVER SWAMP FORESTS

The Congo River supports one of the largest wet forests in the world. Flooded forests cover a region around the river. The Congo swamp forest provides a home to lowland gorillas, chimpanzees, and monkeys. Elephants browse on tall grasses and shrubs. Snakes, frogs, and ever-present insects abound in this tropical swamp. Rare animals living in the region include bonobos, red colobus monkeys, and golden-bellied mangabeys.

▲ Africa's Congo River swamp forests

water may be fresh, salty, or brackish (part freshwater and part salt water).

Swamps support a tremendous variety and quantity of life. Plants range from tiny pondweed and duckweed to soaring bald cypress and tupelo trees. Wildflowers, herbs, grasses, and ferns grow by the thousands in swamp environments.

Swamps are noisy places. Bullfrogs croak, swans trumpet, cranes bugle, and crickets click. The growls of panthers, bears, and alligators mingle with chatter from nesting songbirds. Tall reeds and grasses rattle in the wind.

Bayous are channels or streams of slow-moving water. They connect to swamps and lakes. Only Louisiana, Texas, and Mississippi have bayous. Snakes and alligators glide through **algae**-filled bayou water. Overhead, drapes of Spanish moss hang from knobby-kneed cypress trees.

Saltwater Wetlands

Mangrove swamps, deltas, and tidal marshes are nature's fish farms. Many of the fish caught throughout the world begin life in these waters.

Mangrove swamps can be found along tropical or sub-tropical coastlines, such as those in Florida or Australia. Mangrove trees grow close together, emerging from salty or brackish water. The tree trunk, branches, and leaves form an umbrella over the water. The roots form a complex web below the water's surface. This root network supports snails, mussels, **crustaceans,** and countless numbers of fish eggs and young. Wading birds, such as egrets

▲ Alligators, snakes, and muskrats make their homes in this quiet Louisiana bayou.

> **WATCH IT!**
>
> Learn about Africa's most vibrant wetland region. Watch National Geographic's *Okavango–Africa's Wild Oasis* [ASIN: 6304839723].

> **? WORDS TO KNOW . . .**
>
> **algae (AL-jee)** simple, one-celled plants
>
> **crustaceans (kruhss-TAY-shuhnz)** animals with hard outside shells, such as crabs

▲ A tidal marsh, like this one at Orcas Island, Washington, changes water levels throughout each day.

thousands of seeds. When a delta builds up above the water's surface, grasses and reeds grow. Wading birds, such as the ibis, nest among the grasses and feed along the water's edge. The land is often covered with water when tides roll in.

Tidal marshes lie close to oceans and seas. Tidal marsh water may be fresh, salty, or brackish. Salt marshes form where low-lying land exists along the coastline. Cordgrass, glasswort, and sea lavender sprout in salty marsh soil. These grasses provide habitats for fish and insects to breed. Clams, oysters, crabs, mussels, and most fish humans eat depend on tidal marshes for life.

and roseate spoonbills, dip their bills into the water and feast on the young hiding among the roots.

Deltas form where rivers empty into seas. A typical delta lies at the mouth of the Nile River in Africa, formed at the edge of the Mediterranean Sea. Amid the soil dumped by the river to form the delta are

Chapter Two

Focus on Key Species

✍ At the edge of Florida's Everglades, a snarl of trees forms a peculiar ecosystem called a mangrove swamp. The mangrove plant family here consists of trees that are 100 feet (30 m) tall and shrubs that are shorter than 3 feet (1 m). These strange plants thrive in salt water.

As high tide approaches, salt water rushes through the mangrove swamp. The

▲ Young alligators hide beneath a tangle of mangrove roots.

▲ Beautiful roseate spoonbills use their beaks to scoop food from the marsh muck.

tangled web of mangrove roots provides a safe haven for young fish, sea turtles, and

▲ North America's Everglades National Park

crabs. Slow-moving manatees munch on sea grass. Mullet and snapper weave their way through mangrove roots. Roseate spoonbills and herons dip their heads in search of shrimp and spiny lobsters.

Keystone Species

🦎 A keystone species is any plant or animal that is critical for the survival of other living things within an environment.

Mangrove trees, alligators, and beavers are three keystone species in the wetlands. Each lives in a different ecosystem. Each performs a vital role in nature.

Without the mangrove, the swamp would not exist. The roots harbor the eggs, larvae, and young of dozens of animal species. Wading birds, manatees, fish, and crustaceans feed among the roots.

Alligators live in swamps from South Carolina through Texas. While they are fierce predators, they also create habitats for other creatures. Alligators use their snouts and tails to dig "gator holes" to live in. During droughts,

> 🖱 **LOOK IT UP!**
>
> Learn more about American alligators at the U.S. Fish and Wildlife Service Web site: *http://species.fws.gov/species_accounts/bio_alli.html.*

▲ Alligators were once hunted for their skins. Legal protection saved this fierce predator from extinction.

▲ Long, thin legs allow storks like this one to wade through deep-water marshes and swamps.

alligators rip away tangled water plants. Then sunlight and oxygen are able to reach deeper into the water. Animals living on the swamp bottom get a new chance at life because of alligator landscaping.

Beavers create new wetlands. When beavers build dams across streams, they block water flow. A pond forms behind the beaver dam and often overflows the nearby land. The new habitat encourages waterbirds to nest in the area. Dragonflies and damselflies lay their eggs among the reeds. Herons, cranes, and storks arrive to feed on the insect larvae and tadpoles. Beaver dams change dry stream banks into wetland wonderlands.

these holes are often the last areas with water. Insects, frogs, fish, and crustaceans move in beside the alligators. The holes keep other species alive.

Alligators also clear channels clogged with plant matter. Using their claws and snouts,

Umbrella Species

🐇 An umbrella species is an animal or plant that spreads its legal protection over other creatures. Governments pass laws to protect **endangered** or **threatened** species. Hunting, draining water for crops, filling in wetlands for building, and pollution put wetland plants and animals at risk. Laws protecting animals or plants within these ecosystems protect all creatures that live there.

Giant river otters live in the Pantanal, the world's largest freshwater wetland. Giant river otters need a large hunting territory to catch fish, crustaceans, and small reptiles.

Scientists found poisonous levels of mercury in the water where otters hunt. They fear that the mercury will kill the otters. If pollution is regulated to protect the otters, those rules will also help other species living in the Pantanal. Animals from jabirus to jaguars will share the otters' legal umbrella.

> **? WORDS TO KNOW . . .**
>
> **endangered (en-DAYN-jurd)** on the edge of being completely wiped out; few members of a species still surviving
>
> **threatened (THRET-uhnd)** at risk of becoming endangered

▲ South America's Pantanal

Wood storks like plenty of friends around them when they choose a nesting site.

The Florida black bear makes its home on **hammocks** among cabbage palms and scrub pines. A black bear's range covers from 12 to 115 square miles (31 to 298 sq kilometers). Black bears suffer from loss of habitat. Humans drain marshland and use the land for building or farming. Protecting black bears means restoring their environment. Bears share their habitats with wood storks, red-shouldered hawks, armadillos, raccoons, and wild pigs. A nature preserve that supports black bears protects these other creatures, too.

Birds can also be umbrella species. Central America's great green macaw eats a variety of foods. Feeding takes place in several different places.

Although the macaw's living area is small, its feeding area is extensive. Protecting this species would open a sheltering umbrella over all plants and animals of Central America's lowland wet forests.

Flagship Species

▲ Central America's lowland wet forests

🐇 A flagship species is an attention getter. Flagship species are usually animals, but can also be plants. Pitcher plants and Venus flytraps, two types of **carnivorous** plants, attract plenty of attention. In fact, people try to keep them as houseplants. Pitcher plants and Venus flytraps are rare. They belong in freshwater bogs and fens, not in people's living rooms. Education made people aware of the threat to pitcher plants and flytraps. Laws protect these plants from human collectors.

It is easier to get protection for a flagship species than for a less-appealing species. People would rather save whooping cranes than winged maple-leaf mussels. Yet, both species are endangered.

> **? WORDS TO KNOW . . .**
>
> **carnivorous (kar-NIV-ur-uhss)**
> meat-eating
>
> **📖 READ IT!**
>
> Learn more about plants with a bite in *Carnivorous Plants* by Cynthia Overbeck (Lerner, 1982).

Whooping cranes have been endangered for years. So scientists bred whooping cranes in zoos and protected compounds. They released breeding pairs of cranes into the wild. The whooping crane population has now risen to about 400 birds. A whooper chick born in the wild makes news. When winged mapleleaf mussels produce young, hardly anyone notices.

Indicator Species

Indicator species report on an environment's health. When an indicator species thrives, the ecosystem is healthy. If the species dies or moves away, the ecosystem has problems.

Insects make excellent indicator species. Dragonflies,

▲ This delicate damselfly tells scientists whether a marsh or bog is healthy simply by showing up and laying her eggs.

damselflies, and caddis flies buzz around wetlands, feeding on other insects. A freshwater wetland without one or more of these insects is a sick wetland.

Snails and mussels serve as indicator species in many wetlands, including mangrove swamps. Snails eat algae and other **microscopic** wetland plants. When pollution is too great, algae will not grow. Often a large snail population shows scientists that the water quality is good and that plant quantity is high. Mussels are filter feeders. To eat, they filter food and water through their bodies. When there is too much pollution, the mussels cannot filter properly, and mussel colonies die off. If the water is healthy and food is plentiful, mussel colonies grow.

[Chapter Three]

Predators

❧ At dusk, bats leave their roost to hunt their favorite prey—insects. One bat may eat up to 1,000 insects in an hour. Long-nosed bats sweep through the darkness. A series of sharp chirps echoes over the still waters of South America's Pantanal. The

bats use **echolocation** to find swarms of insects.

About 140 types of bats live in the Amazon and Pantanal wetlands. This is about 25 percent of the mammal species living in the region. The region supports vampire bats that drink blood from animals for food. The most fascinating bat, however, is the greater fishing bat, which scoops fish from the water with its hind legs, just like an eagle. One major difference between fishing bats and fishing birds is that the bats hang upside down to enjoy their feast.

Food Supply

🦎 Wetland predators range from fierce spiders and meat-eating insects to birds, reptiles, and mammals. The number and variety of predators depend on the availability of prey. Predators can be **carnivores** or **omnivores.**

Mammals are the largest wetland predators by size, but not by number. Foxes, lynx, panthers, jaguars,

▲ South America's Pantanal

> **? WORDS TO KNOW . . .**
>
> **carnivores (KAR-nuh-vorz)** animals that eat meat
>
> **echolocation (EK-oh-loh-kay-shuhn)** the process of finding an object by bouncing sound off it to determine its size and distance; used by bats, whales, and dolphins
>
> **omnivores (OM-nuh-vorz)** animals that eat both plants and meat

◀ More than 140 different types of bats thrive in South America's Pantanal.

▲ Clever raccoons can open coolers and garbage cans. They scavenge for food with ease.

wetland animal group. Many insects are carnivores. Mosquitoes and certain fly species are particular predators. They drink blood for food. Their victims are several times larger than they are and do not die from the bites.

Dragonflies, damselflies, and mantises are active wetland predators. The larvae of dragonflies and damselflies live in ponds or standing water. They feed on fish, insect eggs, and tadpoles. Their parents hover over ponds to catch flying insects. Mantises appear to say grace over their meals. They hold their food before them and bow their heads to feed.

raccoons, and otters are mammal hunters in the wetlands. Some predators eat only live animals or freshly killed meat. Others feed on **carrion.**

Insects outnumber every other

Spiders spin elegant webs among tall wetland grasses. The spiny-bellied orb weaver spider weaves a sticky web to catch flying insects. The spider bites its victims and delivers a paralyzing poison.

Wolf spiders do not spin sticky webs. They hunt their food. Wolf spider coloring blends in with their surroundings. They lie in wait for insects to wander past, and then they pounce. Wolf spiders live on every continent except Antarctica.

Birds on the Hunt

Meat-eating birds eat everything from insects to fish to slippery water snakes. Songbirds, such as vireos and swallows, eat insects by the

PROFILE: COTO DOÑANA

Spain's Coto Doñana National Park is a bird sanctuary and a freshwater refuge for many wetland animals. Two endangered predators live in the park: the Spanish lynx and the Spanish imperial eagle. There may be only about 1,000 Spanish lynx left in the world. The park supports about 50. Spanish imperial eagles feed on rabbits living in Coto Doñana. Only 100 to 150 breeding pairs of Spanish imperial eagles survive in the wild today.

▲ Europe's Coto Doñana National Park

thousands. Whippoorwills prefer moths, which they catch in midflight. Major wetland bird predators, however, are usually birds of prey or wading birds.

The most aggressive hunters are birds of prey, such as harriers, eagles, and hawks. Europe's marsh harriers are opportunistic feeders. They take advantage of whatever opportunities arise to eat. If frogs are available, they eat frogs. When mice or ducks come around, they also make tasty meals.

Wetlands support wading bird species, such as cranes, egrets, herons, and storks. Wading birds usually have long legs. Their legs let them walk through shallow water to find food.

The shape of a wading bird's bill suits the type of food the bird eats. Bills can be spoon-shaped, straight, or curved. The roseate spoonbill scoops up small fish, insects, and small crustaceans. Most herons, egrets, and cranes have straight, sharp bills. They peck at fish, frogs, lizards, and snakes hiding among water plants. Curlews have narrow, curved beaks. They step carefully in the shallows and use their bills to pluck worms from wetland mud.

Scaly Hunters

Reptiles such as snakes, snapping turtles, alligators,

> **WATCH IT!**
>
> Wading birds and waterbirds devour many of the Everglades' insects, worms, frogs, and snails. Learn about how they hunt in the Education 2000 video *Birds of the Everglades* [ASIN: B00000IQH3].

A marsh hawk makes a meal of a snow goose. This may seem cruel, but it is all ▶ part of nature's plan.

and crocodiles are successful wetland hunters. Reptiles are cold-blooded and cannot generate body heat on their own. They sun themselves to keep warm. Many reptiles enter the water only to hunt.

Water snakes are generally harmless to humans and are essential to nature. They feed

▲ Marabou storks in Kenya feed on the carcasses of dead flamingos. They are wetland garbage collectors.

! WOULD YOU BELIEVE?

The marabou stork is one of Africa's largest birds. It has a wingspan of 10 feet (3 m). Although it is a wading bird, the marabou stork eats like a vulture or buzzard. It prefers carrion. Only when they are very hungry will marabou storks wade in the water to catch live frogs and snakes.

on rodents, such as water shrews, voles, and swamp rats. Only one North American water snake—the cottonmouth, or water moccasin— is poisonous.

Wetlands also attract ground snakes. They feed on mice, rats, shrews, and voles, as well as frogs, toads, and lizards. Many ground snakes found in wetlands are poisonous. These include rattlesnakes, copperheads, coral snakes, and vipers.

One of the deadliest snakes, South America's ferdelance, slithers through wet forests in the Amazon.

Wetland turtles tend to be omnivores. Snapping turtles prefer fish, but they will hunt water snakes and baby alligators. Some turtles, such as the peninsula cooter, eat meat when they're young and eat plants as adults.

Alligators and crocodiles are the largest and fiercest

▲ Asia's Brahmaputra, Ganges, and Indus rivers

PROFILE: INDIAN GHARIAL

Indian gharials, relatives of crocodiles, are a threatened species. They live in wetlands along the Ganges, Indus, and Brahmaputra rivers. In the 1970s, gharials teetered on extinction. They were hunted for their skins and meat.

Female gharials normally lay 30 to 50 eggs. Only two or three babies from one litter reach adulthood in the wild. To save the gharial from extinction, scientists collected eggs from their nests. They raised young gharials on ranches. They improved the success of a litter from 2 or 3 adults to 30 or 40. Scientists released more than 3,000 gharials in Asian wetlands. Today, several thousand gharials live in the wild.

> **? WORDS TO KNOW . . .**
>
> **extinction (ek-STINGKT-shuhn)**
>
> the state of having no more living members of a species

reptile predators. Most continents have at least one type of crocodile or alligator. The most dangerous crocodile is the Nile crocodile of Africa. These fearsome crocodiles kill more humans each year than lions or tigers.

Cats on the Prowl

Big cats, such as jaguars and panthers, thrive in wetlands. Although many cats dislike water, jaguars are excellent swimmers. When the Amazon rain forest

▲ Nile crocodiles are keystone species throughout African wetlands.

floods, jaguars take to the water to hunt. Florida panthers are endangered in the wild. They live on hammocks in Florida swamps. Florida panthers feed on deer, hogs, raccoons, and armadillos. Fewer than 50 Florida panthers live in the wild.

Bobcats, midsized wildcats, hunt in marshes, bogs, and swamps. They feed on rodents and ground birds. Bobcats hunt at night and, like jaguars, will swim for their supper if necessary.

Successful Predators

Predators that eat a variety of different foods fare better than picky eaters. The apple snail kite may soon become extinct. One of the reasons for

A Florida panther stalks its prey deep ▶ in the Everglades National Park.

▲ Apple snail kites face extinction because they limit their diet to one particular type of snail.

this bird's decreasing numbers is that it eats only one type of snail. When that snail population drops, the kites starve. Compare that to black bears that will eat berries, nuts, seeds, honey, insects, fish, and carrion.

The variety of predators in an area depends on the prey available for them to eat. Insects breed by the millions in wetland environments. That is why so many **insectivores** live in wetlands.

Predators fulfill an important role in nature. Without predators, insects would take over wetlands. Predators also do garbage duty by eating carrion. They maintain a comfortable balance in nature.

? WORDS TO KNOW . . .

insectivores (in-SEKT-uh-vorz)

animals that eat insects

Chapter Four

Prey

A lion stalks a 220-pound (100-kilogram) swamp antelope through the Okavango Delta. The antelope senses the danger. Although he has sharp, curved horns, the antelope would rather flee than fight. Swamp antelopes, or sitatungas, head for deep water when they are in trouble. They are as comfortable in water as they are on land. This time, the antelope escapes the lion but

▲ When this young sitatunga reaches adulthood, it will face dangers from lions on land and from crocodiles in the water.

▲ Africa's Okavango Delta

antelopes, growing up to 4 inches (10 cm). The hooves' shape allows sitatungas to walk over soggy ground. As prey, swamp antelopes are caught between fierce lions of the grasslands and powerful crocodiles in the swamp.

A Well-Stocked Market

Predators have no trouble finding a decent meal in wetland ecosystems. Prey can be bigger than the swamp antelope or smaller than the eye can see. Regardless of size, prey provides needed protein and **nutrients** for predators.

The smallest prey is zooplankton. These microscopic animals drift in water. Zooplankton can be fish or frog eggs, insect larvae, or tiny

runs into a more fearsome predator—the Nile crocodile.

Sitatungas live in African wetlands. They have adapted to swamp life. Swamp antelopes feed mainly on reeds and **papyrus,** which grow in freshwater marshes. Their hooves are much longer than the hooves of other

> **? WORDS TO KNOW . . .**
>
> **nutrients (NOO-tree-uhnts)** substances needed by plants, animals, or humans for growth; key elements of food
>
> **papyrus (puh-PYE-ruhss)** a tall grass that was used to make paper in ancient Egypt and Greece

40

▲ Wood frog tadpoles hide in the safety of marsh grasses.

shrimplike animals. Water insects, beetles, fish, birds, and reptiles feed on zooplankton. Zooplankton live in freshwater, salt water, and brackish water.

Insects make excellent prey as eggs, larvae, and adults. Bats and birds are insect eaters, along with fish, frogs, and small mammals. Some insects, such as dragonflies, can eat their weight in other insects every day.

Mosquitoes, midges, flies, and caddis flies breed by the millions in wetlands. Huge populations are necessary because predators can eat more than 1,000 insects in one feeding.

Frogs are food for predators as eggs, tadpoles, and adults. For a meal, an otter might eat one thousand frog eggs, ten tadpoles, or one adult frog. Female frogs lay thousands of eggs each spring. The

LOOK IT UP!

Learn about the frogs and toads that live in Florida's Corkscrew Swamp. Visit the swamp's Web site at *http://www.audubon.org/local/sanctuary/corkscrew.*

eggs quickly hatch into tadpoles. The growth from tadpole to frog takes about 12 weeks. Luckily, very few eggs survive to adulthood, or every wetland environment would croak from a huge frog population.

Some animals are prey as eggs or young but have few enemies as adults. Alligator, crocodile, and snapping turtle hatchlings fall prey to both land and water animals. Wetland mammals dig up reptile nests and eat the eggs—if they get the chance. Female crocodiles and alligators guard their nests closely. Turtles do not.

When hatchlings emerge from nests, they are in danger. Wading birds, snakes, and fish wait anxiously to feast on the young. Oddly, the same animals that prey on hatchlings might be eaten by the youngster's adult relatives.

Among mammals, rodents

provide food for many larger creatures. Water snakes keep mouse, rat, vole, and shrew populations under control in most wetland ecosystems. Voles and shrews produce several litters of young each season. They reproduce quickly to keep population numbers steady.

Size does not keep prey safe from predators. South American anacondas often catch capybaras, the world's largest rodents, when they drink at the water's edge. Feeding or drinking water leaves victims open to attack.

Good Defenses

Prey have a few defenses against predators. **Camouflage** helps hide prey from their enemies. Praying mantises are leaf green in color. Birds that feed on mantises cannot always see them against green reeds. Bitterns and curlews that live in European marshes have feathers colored like marsh reeds. A nesting bittern is impossible to see unless it moves.

When hiding doesn't work, it's good to run away. Most frogs and toads can hop a good distance when frightened. With luck, they hop out of the reach of their predators.

Freshwater mussels and snails survive because of their hard shells. The shells protect them from many possible predators, but not

> **? WORDS TO KNOW . . .**
>
> **camouflage (KAM-uh-flahzh)** coloring that blends in with the surroundings

◄ An alligator mother protects her young. Few of her hatchlings will survive to become adults.

▲ This round-tailed muskrat keeps a wary eye out for owls and hawks while munching on a meal of marsh reeds.

all of them. Muskrats, raccoons, and herons have no trouble cracking shells to eat the meat inside.

Today's Predator, Tomorrow's Dinner

🐇 Alive or dead, every wetland animal feeds others. Prey may be the eggs, infants, or adults of a species. It can also be the carrion left when animals die. Nature does not waste good food. If food is available, some animal will gnaw, suck, or chomp it. This is true in both freshwater and saltwater environments.

The food cycle depends on prey and predators. Without predators, prey would reproduce in massive numbers. Prey populations would soon take over swamps, wet meadows, fens, and bogs. Predators keep prey population levels in check. This is another example of nature's balance.

Chapter Five

Flora

☞ Formed by glaciers thousands of years ago, the Wingecarribee basin in the mountains of southeast Australia is a peat fen. Over time, it collected peat and runoff water. Peat filtered the water until it was pure. The Australians valued the peat fen as a wetland and as a freshwater **reservoir.**

> **? WORDS TO KNOW . . .**
>
> **reservoir (REZ-ur-vor)** a place for storing water

▲ Wingecarribee was once an active, productive wetland environment.

▲ When the dredge cut through the swamp, it destroyed thousands of years of ecological development.

▲ Australia's Wingecarribee wetland

A machine that cuts peat, called a dredge, lay anchored in the fen's center next to the reservoir. The dredge's platform stood on legs running down into the peat. A buffer zone separated the digging operation from the reservoir. The buffer zone was a natural dam made of thick peat and soil.

In August 1998, heavy rains flooded the fen. The dredge slipped from its anchor. Water and peat pushed the dredge through the buffer zone, carving a channel through the earth. Because it ran on gasoline, the dredge carried pollutants. As water emptied from the wetland into the reservoir, those pollutants entered the pure drinking water system. An ecosystem that had existed for thousands of years was destroyed in a matter of hours.

Freshwater Wetland Plants

Plants play a vital role in establishing a healthy environ-

▲ Ferns make up a large portion of the plant life in Akalai Swamp, a tropical wetland located in Hawaii.

▲ Papyrus, a woody grass, has been used as paper and lashed into rafts or boats. Papyrus provides a safe haven for marsh young.

? WORDS TO KNOW . . .

biomes (BYE-ohmz) large ecosystems in which the plants and animals are adapted to a particular climate or physical environment

growing seasons. The plant life can grow so thick that humans can barely cut their way through it. Temperate wetlands support plants that survive freezing winters and bloom in hot summers. Tundra wetlands teem with plants that hug the ground to protect themselves from the constantly cold temperatures.

Wetlands may have water only part of the year. Prairie potholes are seasonal ecosystems where plants grow until the water disappears. Other wetlands, such as swamps and fens, are always underwater. Cattails, bulrushes, and papyrus roots and stems are always covered with water.

Wetland **biomes** have three types of plants: emer-

ment. The amount and variety of plant life in a wetland ecosystem depends on the climate. Tropical wetlands have year-round gent, submergent, and free-floating. Emergent plant roots and lower stems lie under-water. Their branches, upper stems, and leaves live above water. Submergent plants live completely underwater. They may send shoots above water to produce seeds. Free-floating plants are plants with no fixed roots. They float on the water's surface.

Emergent Wetland Plants

Emergent plants grow in every type of wetland. Most plants in temporary wetlands, such as prairie potholes, are emergent plants. Emergent plants include grasses, ferns, wildflowers, and trees.

Emergent grasses can be thin, green stalks, such as marshfinger grass. They can also be thick and woody, such as papyrus or bamboo. Cane, bul-rushes, and reeds grow in freshwater wetlands. Salt grass, spike grass, and cordgrass thrive in salt water or tidal marshes.

Not every bit of wetland soil is under inches of water. Some soil may just be spongy and damp. Typically, ferns grow in this spongy, moist soil. They do not produce flowers or seeds, but instead they reproduce by spores. Ferns can be tiny and look like moss. Or they can grow as tall as trees. Tree ferns

> **! WOULD YOU BELIEVE?**
>
> Wetland wildflowers can have strange names. Green adder's mouth looks like an open snake's mouth. Pussy toes are soft and furry. Beard tongue is a furry, tongue-shaped flower. Beggar-ticks, Dutchman's-breeches, green dragon, and lizard's tail also decorate North American wetlands.

PROFILE: HERBS OF THE WETLANDS

Native Americans often used wetland herbs to cure sickness or fix wounds. They made herbal remedies to stop bleeding, treat burns, ease headaches, or take the itch out of bites. They crushed leaves and bark and soaked them in hot water to make healing tea. Knowledgeable medicine men and women ground dried leaves with bear or duck grease to make ointments. Native herbalists knew how to use everything from Spanish moss to skunk cabbage to cure health problems.

> **! WOULD YOU BELIEVE?**
>
> When in a wetland ecosystem, remember the rhyme, "Leaves of three, beware of me." Avoid plants with clusters of three leaves on a stem. You may be touching poison ivy, poison oak, or poison sumac. All three give humans itchy rashes.

grow in Australia and South America. Common wetland ferns include adder's-tongue and maidenhair fern.

Hundreds of wildflowers paint wetlands with brilliant colors. Blue flag or yellow flag irises, Queen Anne's lace, and pink marshmallow dance in soft summer winds. Cattails bob up and down at the water's edge. Daisies, goldenrod, dandelions, and buttercups sprinkle yellow amid the rich greens of wet meadows.

Knobby-kneed bald cypress trees fare well in freshwater swamps. Willows and alders edge freshwater marshes. Evergreens such as magnolias, hollies, cedars, and pines grow well in wetland

Spanish moss hangs from a bald ▶ cypress tree in a Louisiana swamp.

environments of the south-eastern United States.

Freshwater Submergent Plants

Submergent plants live underwater. Their roots, stems, and leaves produce food under the water's surface. Some submergent plants send shoots above the water level when it is time to produce flowers and seeds.

Freshwater submergent plants include bladderwort, water milfoil, and hydrilla.

WOULD YOU BELIEVE?

Some plants are both male and female. Coontail is a free-floating submergent plant that bears both male and female flowers. When it is time to reproduce, the **stamens** release from the male flowers. The stamens rise to the surface and open. Their pollen fertilizes the female flowers. Seeds form and are carried by the water. New colonies of coontail begin without the parent plant ever breaking the water's surface.

? WORDS TO KNOW . . .

stamens (STAY-muhnz) the pollen-producing parts of a flower

Bladderworts eat meat—or rather, they dissolve insects. When water insects or larvae touch the hairs around the plant's bladders, the plant sucks the prey inside. The bladderwort takes needed nutrients from its prey.

Alien or non-native water plants create serious problems in wetlands. Two such North American exotics, or aliens, are milfoil and hydrilla. Milfoil comes from Europe, Asia, and northern Africa. Milfoil grows quickly and chokes off the growth of native water plants. Within a short time, milfoil fills a pond completely, blocking sun from other plants and making water travel impossible. The plant cover kills other native plants, fish, and animals within the pond. Animals and insects that depend on pond life suffer from loss of habitat. Because milfoil has no natural enemies in North America, it is difficult to control once it begins growing in wetland areas.

Hydrilla is a common freshwater aquarium plant. The plant entered North American wetlands when people washed out their aquariums. Hydrilla passed through the sewer systems and into wetlands. Like milfoil, hydrilla

A dredge scoops hydrilla and water lilies from Lake Okechobee, Florida. The weeds ▶ clog the lake and kill other plant life.

took over. Some scientists suggest introducing grass carp to eat hydrilla. The important question is, what will eat the grass carp when it starts to grow out of control?

Floating Plants

Floating plants have no attached roots. They include duckweed, pondweed, water hyacinth, and mosquito fern. Floating plants live in all types of water. They are found throughout the world. **Phytoplankton,** the

> **? WORDS TO KNOW . . .**
>
> **phytoplankton (fie-toe-PLANGK-tuhn)** one-celled floating water plants, such as algae or diatoms

▲ Freshwater snails like the one shown here feed on phytoplankton.

👁 **WATCH IT!**

Discover the animals living among the roots of swamp trees. Watch National Geographic's *Creatures of the Mangrove* [ASIN: 6304474571].

smallest water plants, live in both freshwater and salt water.

Phytoplankton forms the foundation for food webs in all wetlands. Zooplankton, snails, mussels, and clams feed on phytoplankton. Every larger animal that lives in a wetland ecosystem eats food that can be traced back to phytoplankton.

Saltwater Wetland Plants

☙ Tidal wetlands have changes in water level twice daily. The tide comes in and out roughly every 12 hours. A mangrove swamp flourishes under in-again-out-again water. The regular flow of new salt water helps to cleanse the swamp.

Coastal wetlands support several grasses, such as eel-grass, redhead, and wigeon grass. Not true grasses, these plants belong to different families. Saltwater grasses provide habitats for small fish and crabs, insect larvae, and fish eggs. They feed ducks, geese, and swans.

PROFILE: MOSQUITO FERN

Mosquito fern drifts in freshwater ponds, lakes, and wetlands of North America. Like duckweed and algae, mosquito fern forms a living blanket over still freshwater. In autumn, the fern changes from brownish green to deep rust red. In winter, mosquito fern lies inactive on the wetlands' floor. In spring, ferns rise to the surface. They produce a new crop of mosquito fern to spread over the water.

(continued),

Chapter Six

Herbivores

A Chinese water deer doe delivers four fawns in late spring. Water deer can have a litter of up to six fawns. Most other types of deer produce only one or two fawns per year. The doe hides her fawns among the marsh reeds. The fawns' brown-and-white coats blend in perfectly. They are invisible to predators.

▲ Water deer habitat in eastern Asia

Chinese water deer are **herbivores.** Although they generally feed on reeds, grasses, and leaves, they also eat crops. Rice paddies, wheat fields, and even carrot patches are not safe from hungry water deer. Chinese farmers think the deer are pests.

Water deer live in swamps, stands of marsh reeds, and grasslands of northern China and Korea. The deer now also live in the wetlands of England and France. The English-based Chinese water deer herds were created when captured deer escaped from wildlife parks.

Large Plant Eaters

🐇 Deer of all types are among the largest herbivores in wetland environments. North America's white-tailed deer live in forests, grasslands, swamps, wet meadows, and fens. They feed on grasses, leaves, and, in times of great hunger, tree bark.

Other large wetland herbivores

❓ WORDS TO KNOW . . .

herbivores (HUR-buh-vorz)

animals that eat plants

❗ WOULD YOU BELIEVE?

Chinese water deer have no antlers, but they do have tusks. Males grow tusks about 2 inches (5 cm) long. Female tusks are much smaller. The tusks are used as weapons when males fight for the right to mate with a doe.

◄ Chinese water deer make pests out of themselves by eating farmers' crops.

PROFILE: BAMBI GONE BERSERK

In the 1700s, southern U.S. coastal colonists hunted white-tailed deer nearly to extinction. Limited deer hunting became law. This was the first attempt in North America to save an endangered species.

Then, humans made a big mistake. Throughout the South, humans killed off the major deer predators. Without wolves or cougars, the white-tailed deer population exploded. In coastal wetlands and swamps, deer have become a plague. They actually eat away the balance nature provides between plants and animals. Hunting cannot reduce the deer numbers sufficiently. Only natural predators—and plenty of them—can get the situation under control.

▲ Moose are among the largest plant eaters in the wetlands.

include moose, elk, and Chincoteague ponies. These herbivores graze on grasses, reeds, and tender leaves. Moose wade into lakes and rivers to browse. Chincoteague ponies are wild. They are the distant relatives of tame ponies

[Herbivores]

▲ Europe's Camargue Regional Nature Park

that were released or escaped several hundred years ago.

In Asia, water buffaloes wallow in wetland mud. They feed on reeds, bulrushes, and water grasses. Water buffaloes rarely move far from these areas.

Malaysia's bearded pigs don't bother picking fruit for themselves. They follow monkeys through the mangrove swamps. The monkeys drop

PROFILE: FRANCE'S CAMARGUE REGIONAL NATURE PARK

Southern France boasts a stunning, vital wetland environment called the Camargue. The Camargue is a delta wetland that was formed where the Rhone River empties into the Mediterranean Sea. About 12,000 greater flamingos arrive each year to breed in the Camargue. The females build mud mounds on islands in the park. The birds lay only one egg. When they lift off in flight, they fill the sky with shades of pink and coral. The flamingos share their winter retreat with thousands of mallards, widgeons, and shovelers. Nutria, grass snakes, and viperine snakes live on land where French farmers plant rice. Much of this vast wetland has been turned into rice fields or cattle pastures.

▲ Malaysia in southeast Asia

READ IT!

Step into the swamp! Read Theresa Greenaway's *Swamp Life* (Dorling Kindersley, 1993) and get a close-up view of the swamp ecosystem.

partially eaten fruit, which becomes a quick meal for Malaysia's bearded pigs.

Herbivores do not just graze on grass and leaves. They also eat the fruits of plants: berries, seeds, nuts, and nectar. The Amazon's hoatzin bird feeds on fruit and flowers. Africa's red colobus monkey eats fruit and leaves in its Congo River swamp forest home.

Hummingbirds dart among wetland wildflowers, feasting on the flowers' sweet nectar. Several kinds of bats eat only fruit or nectar. Swamp rats like seeds and berries along with their normal meal of stems and leaves. Meadow voles can be found hunting for seeds and roots in most wet meadows and prairie potholes.

Many wetland birds feed on seeds, berries, and insects. Cardinals, goldfinches, and pine siskins mainly eat seeds. They all eat insects, too. Indigo buntings dine mainly on insects but peck seeds and berries off the ground.

Most people recognize beavers, squirrels, and rabbits. Beavers create wetland ecosystems and feed there as well. They eat leaves and tender branches, along with river reeds. Gray squirrels can live anywhere trees grow. They thrive in swamps where nuts, berries, fruit, and seeds are plentiful. Cottontail and

PROFILE: RUBY-THROATED HUMMINGBIRD

The ruby-throated hummingbird feeds on the nectar of flowers in woods, gardens, swamps, and wet meadows. These tiny hummingbirds weigh only about 1 ounce (28 grams) but migrate nearly 2,000 miles (3,200 km) each year. Ruby-throated hummingbirds eat twice their weight in nectar each day, mostly from red flowers.

▲ Northern shoveler ducks migrate to the North American tundra from the south each
spring. The Migratory Bird Act of 1918 protects them on their journey.

marsh rabbits nibble their way through grass and wildflowers. Clover is a favorite food of rabbits.

Swans, geese, and many ducks eat water plants, seeds, and roots. Baby swans, called cygnets, feed on worms and insect larvae as infants, but they eat mostly plants as adults.

Omnivores

Although many omnivores are considered predators, some prefer plants. Surprisingly, many bears eat far more plant matter than meat. More than 75 percent of the black bear's diet consists of fruit, nuts, seeds, and honey. Grizzly bears, known for eating salmon, actually eat more berries, roots, nuts, and leaves. Bears in a feeding frenzy can eat 200,000 berries in only one day.

Saltwater Plant Feeders

Some animals living among the mangrove roots and salt marsh grasses are **detrivores** or herbivores. Dead mangrove leaves and branches fall into the salt water of the swamp. This dead matter is called **detritus.** Detritus is the foundation for the food web within the swamp. Snails, shrimp, and crabs that eat the detritus grow and become food for larger fish, crabs, and birds.

> **? WORDS TO KNOW . . .**
>
> **detritus (deh-TRY-tuhs)** dead plant or animal material or organic waste
>
> **detrivores (deh-TRY-vorz)** animals that eat dead or rotting matter

▲ Fierce-looking fiddler crabs spend their days dining on scraps of seaweed.

Butterflies and beetles feed on the live leaves and bark. They are food for a host of birds and spiders living among the mangroves.

Fiddler crabs may be the most interesting of the tidal salt marsh herbivores. With their big claws, they look fierce and threatening. However, these scuttling crustaceans actually thrive on bits of seaweed and algae caught among marsh grasses.

Chapter Seven

A Cycle of Life

🐍 Night has fallen, and a snake is on the hunt. The snake skims through a Louisiana bayou with its head raised above the water. It is a cottonmouth—a deadly poisonous snake.

Tonight, the cottonmouth hunts a swamp rat. The rat is

▲ A cottonmouth slithers through a Louisiana bayou in search of a meal.

NORTH AMERICA

Louisiana
Bayou
Country

Atlantic
Ocean

Gulf of
Mexico

0   250 Miles
0   250 KM

▲ North America's Louisiana bayou country

changes as small as 2° to 3° Fahrenheit (1° Celsius).

The rat takes a drink at the water's edge. The cottonmouth lunges forward. It sinks its fangs into the rat's body, and the fangs inject poison. Then the snake releases its prey.

The swamp rat tries to flee. It heads into thick grasses along the bayou's banks. It is too late. The rat dies quickly from the poison. The snake follows its prey by scent. Coming upon the rat's body, the cottonmouth touches the rat with its tongue. One touch assures the snake that its prey is dead. Cottonmouths eat only dead prey, which they swallow headfirst.

warm-blooded, and the snake has no trouble locating the rat in the dark. It senses the rat's body heat. Cottonmouths, also called water moccasins, have built-in thermometers. Temperature sensors lie in pits between their eyes. These snakes can sense temperature

▲ Snakes are cold-blooded. They enjoy sunning themselves on rocks on a hot afternoon.

Breeding Season

🐾 A female cottonmouth slithers through the reeds lining the bayou. She is fully grown, measuring 2 feet (.6 m) long. Her back is dark olive, and her belly is a paler yellow. It is spring, and the female is ready to breed. Cottonmouths normally breed every two years. The female finds a male cotton-

mouth. The pair will mate, but then will probably never see each other again.

The female carries her young inside her body for three to four months. She produces 10 live young. Normal cottonmouth females deliver

🖱 LOOK IT UP!

Most people confuse the poisonous cottonmouth with other harmless water snakes. Visit these Web sites and learn more about water snakes in North American wetlands: *http://www. uga.edu/srelherp/snakes/ novenom_2.htm* and *http://www.southalley.com/ album_nerodia.html*.

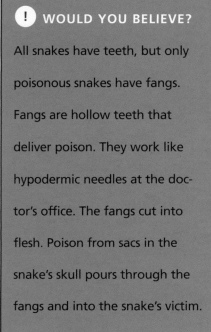

? **WORDS TO KNOW . . .**

juvenile (JOO-vuh-nile)
young, not yet having reached adulthood

from one to twelve young.

At birth, the young snakes are about 9 inches (23 cm) long. Their bodies are almost as wide as a nickel. Young cottonmouths have bright-colored, coppery bands on their backs. Their tails can be yellow or yellow-green. As the snakes grow, their body colors change from orange to dull olive or black.

From birth, **juvenile** cottonmouths hunt their own food. They shake their pale yellow-green tails in the air, attracting small frogs or fish. Their prey mistakes the shaking tails for worms or caterpillars. The young snakes are already able to inject prey with venom when they are born.

Juveniles keep a wary eye out for predators. While cottonmouths are small, owls, hawks, eagles, snapping turtles, and alligators prey on them. Adult snakes, including other cottonmouths, also eat young water moccasins.

Cottonmouth Characteristics

Cottonmouths are the only venomous water snakes in North America. The snake gets its nickname from the snow white lining of its mouth. A cottonmouth will often coil its body into a spiral. It leans its head back and opens its mouth wide, displaying the white lining.

Female Cottonmouths

🐍 Female snakes do not make good mothers. Once their

> **! WOULD YOU BELIEVE?**
>
> Relatives of the cottonmouth are found in Central America, Asia, and Europe.

▲ Juvenile cottonmouths have to be on their guard if they don't want predators like this short-eared owl to swoop down and catch them.

▲ It is easy to see how this fierce cottonmouth got its name. Its mouth is lined in white.

children are born, they abandon them. The young must fend for themselves against predators.

The cottonmouth female of the bayou has lost most of her litter to predators. Only one snake survives to adulthood. It feeds on fish, frogs, lizards, birds, mice, rats, and other snakes. Cottonmouths eat their food whole. Their bodies easily digest fur, feathers, and bones.

The surviving snake is a female. She grows quickly and soon stretches 4 feet (1.2 m) long. As she grows, she sheds her tight, too-small skin. She slithers around a tree branch or over a rough rock to remove the old skin. In the past year, she has shed her skin four times.

During the day, cotton-mouths sun themselves on warm rocks or tree branches. Snakes are cold-blooded. They cannot keep themselves warm and must rely on the sun for body heat. As night approaches, the female snake slips from her warm perch into the water to hunt.

Our female escaped eagles, king snakes, and largemouth bass during her life. She slipped past great blue herons and snapping turtles. Unfortunately, she could not escape disease. Her body carries **parasites.** They have infected her lungs. She has also developed ulcers, or open sores, in her stomach and intestines. The parasites and

DON'T DO IT!

Don't risk a bite from a water moccasin. If you see one, keep your distance. Do not try to catch it. Don't throw rocks at it or poke it with a stick. These snakes may attack. If you are bitten, go to a hospital immediately.

WORDS TO KNOW . . .

parasites (PA-ruh-sites) animals that live on or in another animal in order to feed off of it

71

▲ When a cottonmouth dies, it becomes food for fly maggots and other insect larvae.

ulcers bring the cottonmouth to an early death.

She dies at the water's edge. Her body is now food for carrion feeders. Insects lay eggs on her flesh. Birds peck at the meat, carrying tender scraps to their young. Nutrients from the rotting flesh sink into the ground. They feed the plants that hid the cottonmouth while she lived. This is the wetland cycle of life.

The Land of Trembling Earth

A mother black bear and her cubs step carefully on a hammock in the depths of the swamp. She knows by instinct that this "land" within the swamp will shake beneath her weight. Though this island supports the growth of black

▲ Step into the land of the trembling earth—the Okefenokee Swamp.

gum trees and loblolly bays, it is not true land. It is a massive peat island, floating in the deep brown waters. It is called the Okefenokee, named by the Creek, an American Indian tribe, and it means "the land of trembling earth."

High above, long-legged wood storks squawk and flutter as they build their nests. Wood storks are not territorial. They happily live within a few feet of other nesting pairs. This black gum has more than a dozen wood stork nests, stacked one above another like apartments.

Georgia's Okefenokee Swamp is North America's largest swamp. It covers about 496,000 acres (200,700 hectares). Roughly 70 islands emerge above the dark water. Within the swamp, a variety of habitats exist. Among these ecosystems are pond cypress forests, evergreen forests, black gum forests, wet prairies, shrub wetlands, and floating peat islands.

Most water in the Okefenokee Swamp comes from rain and runoff. The **watershed** that feeds the

▲ North America's Okefenokee Swamp

74

▲ Okefenokee water is pure and drinkable—even if it is the color of strong tea.

swamp covers more than 1,400 square miles (3,626 sq km). Precipitation in the region usually adds up to 50 inches (127 cm) a year, and most is from rainfall. In many places, people could easily wade through the water, because it is rarely more than 2 feet (.6 m) deep. Of course, waders would be sharing space with alligators and poisonous water moccasins.

Okefenokee's peat is the result of thousands of years of dead water lilies and pieces of cypress trees. The peat is thick, solid, and floating. It dyes the water a deep brown, just like dark tea. The water is exceptionally pure because the peat "brew" makes it acidic. Mold, mildew, and spores cannot grow in or pollute the water. Only acid-loving plants can survive in this water.

Living in the Swamp

🦎 Okefenokee supports more than 600 species of plants and 425 species of animals. The dominant plant is the cypress tree. Pond cypress and bald cypress rise above the swamp, shading the land and water below. Their knobby trunks may represent nearly 500 years of growth. Cypress trees are related to conifers (cone-bearing trees), but unlike conifers, they shed their needles each year.

In other regions of the swamp, loblolly bay grows beside spiky, dark green holly. Slash pines drop their needles, creating a rust brown carpet on the earth below. Climbing heath and

◄ Wax myrtle and cypress loom above the hammocks of the swamp.

greenbriar snake their way up tree trunks.

In the wet prairies, water lilies pave a white-and-yellow road amid tea brown water. Golden club and yellow-fringed orchids add a touch of sun to the swamp's gloom. Pickerel-weed emerges from the water. On clumps of damp earth, swamp iris open their delicate petals of blue and yellow.

Not all Okefenokee plants are lovely or safe. There is poison ivy nestled next to deep purple violets. Feathery poison sumac waves in the gentle Georgia breezes.

Insects should be wary. The Okefenokee supports four types of carnivorous plants: pitcher plants, sundews, butterworts, and bladderworts.

▲ Pitcher plants do not actually eat their prey; they digest the nutrients from the prey's body.

Pitcher plants attract insects into their cup-shaped flowers. Once inside, there is no exit. Insects are digested by plant

🖱 **LOOK IT UP!**

Learn more about the Okefenokee Swamp. Access this Web site: *http://www. sherpaguides.com/georgia/ okefenokee_swamp/index.html.*

▲ The sundew's glue-covered hairs hold fast to insects they catch.

Okefenokee Animal Life

✏ Birds make up the majority of the animals in the swamp. About 235 species live full- or part-time in the Okefenokee. The largest bird there is the sandhill crane. With their 7-foot (2.1-m) wingspans, sandhills make a dramatic picture in flight. Sandhills stand 4 feet (1.2 m) tall. Their height allows them to see approaching danger. These cranes trumpet an alarm that has earned them the nickname "watchmen of the swamp."

juices. Sundews and butter-worts use a gluey substance to hold on to their prey. Blad-derworts live and feed beneath the water. They have small openings into their bladders that act like trapdoors.

Wading birds spend their swamp days bobbing their heads up and down in the shallow water. They peck in the muck for crustaceans, frogs, toads, snakes, and

Great egrets nearly became extinct when the birds were killed so that their ▶ feathers could be collected for ladies' hats.

insects. Two common species among swamp wading birds are the white ibis and the great egret. White ibises are noted for their sharp curved bills and long orange-pink legs. White ibises feed on insects and crayfish. The great egret hunts fish, frogs, and snakes.

These noble white birds once suffered greatly from human activities. Their beautiful feathers were used as decorations for women's hats. Unfortunately, the feather collectors usually killed the feather producers, which seriously reduced the egret population.

Each night, the Okefenokee chorus gathers to present a concert. The pig frog opens the night's entertainment with a few piglike grunts. The river frog snores. The bullfrog croaks. Male leopard frogs sound much like the squeak of hands squeezing the open end of a balloon. The green tree frog joins in with its honk, while the barking tree frog yelps like a dog pack. Add to that the banjolike notes of the bronze frog and the charming tones of the southern toad. High notes and low, loud notes and soft, the frog and toad choruses sing the music of the swamp—and the concert is free for any who choose to listen.

Protective laws and fashion changes have given the egret population an opportunity to grow.

Osprey, owls, and vultures hunt their food in Okefenokee. Osprey feed on fish, which they find easily enough in swamp waters. About 36 types of fish swim in Okefenokee's waters. Owls prefer hunting at night. The barred owl ruffles its feathers, then swoops down to catch rats, mice, or ground birds. Vultures perform a needed service. They eat dead flesh. In this way, they clean dead animal bodies from the land.

Migratory ducks and geese arrive in Okefenokee in time to spend a mild winter there. When spring

▲ There is a risk that Okefenokee's white-tailed deer population may grow too large for the swamp to support it.

comes, they fly north to nest and breed.

About 50 types of mammals inhabit the swamp. The largest is the Florida black bear. This small cousin to the grizzly grows to about 300 pounds (136 kg). White-tailed deer also thrive in the Okefenokee, as there are no major predators to slow their numbers.

Otters and raccoons provide a bit of humor for

▲ A river otter takes time from his play to enjoy a sip of water.

can open any cooler with ease and will take anything from peanut butter to ham sandwiches.

No swamp would be complete without an array of reptiles. The Okefenokee reptile population is led by about 10,000 alligators. Once hunted for their skins, these fierce predators have been protected by law for many years. Alligators are basically shy and have no interest in humans—with one exception. A mother alligator protects her eggs from all creatures, regardless of size. Females will attack humans, bears, raccoons, or sandhill cranes in defense of their young.

The swamp supports more than two dozen species of

swamp tourists. Finding an otter is easy—just look for a mudslide into the water. Otters are fun and frisky. They love playing in the water and can swim quite fast. Raccoons, like bears, eat anything. This includes campers' food supplies. Raccoons have agile hands and clever minds. They

snakes. Most are harmless, but not all. The largest and most deadly is the water moccasin, or cottonmouth. Coral snakes and eastern diamondback rattlesnakes are the other poisonous members of the swamp. One of the most stunning swamp snakes is the rainbow snake. Its black body gleams in the sun, along with brilliant red stripes and a yellow underbelly.

Threats to the Okefenokee Swamp

❧ Many years ago, natural fires that were started by lightning strikes plagued the swamp. People living near the swamp feared the loss of their homes and farm crops. The answer to their problem was to build the Suwannee River Sill, an earthen dam that holds water in the swamp. It raises the swamp's water level and supposedly prevents fires because the fires cannot jump from place to place. Surprisingly, swamps are a mix of wet ground, underwater ground,

This rainbow snake is not poisonous, but many ▶ other local snakes carry a venom-packed bite.

and dry hammocks. The more dry stuff, the easier it is to spread fires. The sill seemed like a good idea.

Over the years, the earthen dam was expanded and strengthened with concrete. The swamp's water has naturally high levels of acid. That acid has eaten away at the sill's concrete and steel water controls. Today, the sill has acid-burned holes the size of dinner plates. Water leaks through the holes and creates strong currents. Experts disagree on whether to repair or remove the sill. However, both sides agree that human interference will change the nature of this valued wetland environment.

On one side of the swamp known as Trail Ridge, the Du Pont Corporation holds the rights to mine land rich in titanium. Titanium is used to make titanium oxide. This compound whitens toothpaste (and your teeth). It is also used to produce plastic products and print the letters on M&M candies.

Du Pont wants to mine the land for this valuable mineral over a 50-year period. Over time, the company would develop new pine-and-grass wetlands on the used land. Ecologists feel that mining of any kind will result in permanent damage to the swamp.

Two rare or endangered species that live in the swamp—the indigo snake and the gopher tortoise—may be hurt by the mining. The gopher

▲ The gopher tortoise digs burrows that burrowing owls, foxes, opossums, raccoons, skinks, and snakes will later live in.

tortoise digs its burrows along Trail Ridge. The gopher tortoise is Georgia's state reptile. It is also a keystone species of the region. Its burrows are homes for burrowing owls, foxes, opossums, raccoons, gopher frogs, red-tailed skinks, diamondback rattlers, and eastern indigo snakes. Ecologists hope that the survival of these creatures will be considered before actions damage the delicate swamp ecosystem.

The Human Touch

🦎 The mangrove and swamp forests of Vietnam stood for thousands of years in Asia. Salt water washed in and out. Fish spawned and produced young.

In the 1960s and 1970s, war raged between North Vietnam and South Vietnam. A chemical was used to kill plant life throughout the area. That chemical, Agent Orange, was highly effective. The war

destroyed nearly half of the mangrove swamps in the Mekong Delta.

The chemical did not go away. **Monsoons** came, and rain poured through the jungles. Runoff and groundwater carried Agent Orange into the mangrove swamps. The chemical did its job, and the mangrove died. Today, more than 30 years later, attempts to replant the swamps still fail. The success of Agent Orange continues long after the war ended.

Threats to Wetlands

🐇 Major threats to wetlands come from chemical pollution, sewage, industrial pollution, human activity, and alien species. In areas where humans continue to cut trees for timber, erosion has also become a serious threat.

Fertilizers, plant killers, and pest killers can be used hundreds of miles away and still affect an ecosystem. Chemicals enter wetlands through runoff or groundwater.

▲ Asia's Mekong Delta

> **? WORDS TO KNOW . . .**
>
> **monsoons (mon-SOONZ)**
>
> winds that reverse direction with the seasons

> **📖 READ IT!**
>
> Wetlands are disappearing. Learn about how these vital ecosystems can be saved in Anita Louise McCormick's *Vanishing Wetlands* (Lucent Books, 1995).

◄ U.S. Air Force planes spray Agent Orange on wetlands along the Mekong River.

DO IT!

Reduce chemical runoff from your home. Use biodegradable cleaners and detergents because they can be broken down naturally and are less harmful to the environment than non-biodegradable cleaners. Keep raked leaves and grass clippings out of storm drains.

Although wetland plants and soil can filter out some of the pollution, humans produce far more pollution than can be cleaned.

Plant and pest killers remain poisonous long after their original use. These chemicals travel through the water cycle. Plant killer used in Orlando, Florida, can kill sawgrass in the Everglades, which is several hundred miles to the south. Pest killers destroy harmful weevils and locusts but also kill butterflies, dragonflies, and praying mantises. The poison that kills insects gets into the bodies of insect eaters. Collected poisons can eventually affect birds of prey, large fish, mammals, and even humans.

People Problems

Every swamp, bog, and fen serves a purpose. Each one helps clean our environment. Unfortunately, many wetlands lie on land humans want.

People discovered many years ago that they could fill in wetlands with dirt and use the land. Some wetlands have been turned into farms or cattle ranches. Others are now housing developments, golf courses, and vacation resorts.

In the 1600s, the land covered by the lower 48 states held 220 million acres (89 million hectares) of wetlands. These ranged from massive

▲ A bulldozer fills a wetland with topsoil. In a few months, this swamp will be a housing development.

swamps to temporary potholes and playas, which are dry riverbeds of ponds that hold water only part of the year. Today, wetlands in the continental United States span about 105 million acres (42 million hectares). Of those, about 58,000 acres (23,000 hectares) are filled, drained, dredged, tilled, mined, grazed, and polluted each year. Programs to rebuild wetlands cannot keep up with projects that destroy them.

The loss of wetlands to farms, housing, and recreation is a worldwide problem. Many people want a beachside home, but few realize the heavy toll that results. Animals and plants lose their habitats. The land can no longer clean itself, so pollution increases. About 40 percent of freshwater in the United States is too polluted to drink. Many wetlands no longer support fish or plant life. Similar situations exist everywhere people live.

People need to stop destroying wetlands and begin rebuilding them. Wetlands have been set aside as nature preserves, national parks, and protected habitats. Wetlands also can be used to clean water naturally, cheaply, and effectively. Some countries have found it cheaper to rebuild a wetland than to build a new sewage treatment plant. Australia manages more than a dozen wetland water treatment centers.

Strangers

Alien species have become a worldwide problem. Non-native species arrive from other places and take over

◂ A biologist examines a Louisiana swamp for industrial pollution.

their new homes. Worldwide travel, shipping, and business have expanded alien species problems. Some alien water plants have entered wetlands through sewer systems. Aquarium plants flushed down the toilet can seriously damage wetlands.

Once an alien species settles in, it is hard to contain. Bringing in predators to attack the invaders just creates new problems. An endless cycle of introducing more predators takes hold.

Alien species with no natural enemies throw off nature's balance. Consider the situation of two species alien to North American wetlands: nutria and milfoil. Nutria are enough like beavers to be eaten by the

▲ Nutria may be alien species, but they do not harm their bayou environment.

beaver's natural predators. Milfoil creates serious problems because it has no natural enemies. The best answer is to reduce the occurrence of alien species in wetlands. If not, already endangered wetlands will die.

Chart of Species

CONTINENT	KEYSTONE SPECIES	FLAGSHIP SPECIES	UMBRELLA SPECIES	INDICATOR SPECIES
AFRICA	Nile crocodiles, hippopotamuses, papyrus, marsh grasses	purple herons, glossy ibises, shoebill storks	Nile crocodiles, hippopotamuses, various wetland raptors	mussels, snails, clams, dragon-flies, caddis flies
ASIA	marsh grasses, ducks, geese	pitcher plants, glossy ibises, Eurasian spoonbills, purple herons, Eurasian golden plovers	Eurasian spoonbills, glossy ibises, various wetland raptors, Eurasian golden plovers	mussels, snails dragonflies, damselflies, caddis flies
AUSTRALIA	peat moss, mangroves, red crabs	pitcher plants, black swans, glossy ibises	black swans, glossy ibises, various wetland raptors	mussels, snails, dragonflies, caddis flies
EUROPE	peat moss, marsh grasses, ducks, geese, beavers	beavers, Eurasian spoonbills, purple herons, old world pelicans, Eurasian golden plovers	beavers, Eurasian spoonbills, Eurasian golden plovers, various wetlands raptors	mussels, snails, dragonflies, damselflies, caddis flies
NORTH AMERICA	mangroves, alligators, marsh grasses, beavers, lesser snow geese, American crocodiles	pitcher plants, Venus flytraps, whooping cranes, trumpeter swans, American crocodiles	alligators, Florida panthers, whoop-ing cranes, various wetland raptors	mussels, snails, clams, dragon-flies, damselflies, caddis flies
SOUTH AMERICA	mangroves, water lilies, hoatzins, greater flamingos	hoatzins, greater flamingos, giant river otters	giant river otters, macaws, anacondas	mussels, snails, dragonflies, caddis flies

▲ The above chart gives a starting point for identifying key species. Each wetland environment has its own key species. The above chart lists some of those species.

[Bold-faced entries are the ones discussed in the text.]